Al

When you
need to speak and
you're all alone, write it
down, it will be heard
thru-out eternity —

Love you always

Robins + Rainbows
Tea Bags
&
candles

Michele

Our dreams are as real as we believe them to be.
This is a journal of hopes and visions.

....
(name)

....
(date)

ISBN 0-7683-2047-X

Text by Flavia and Lisa Weedn

Illustrations by Flavia Weedn

© Weedn Family Trust

www.flavia.com

All rights reserved.

Published in 1998 by Cedco Publishing Company.

100 Pelican Way, San Rafael, California 94901

For a free catalog of other Cedco® products, please write

to the address above, or visit our website: www.cedco.com

Printed in Hong Kong

3 5 7 9 10 8 6 4 2

The artwork for each picture is digitally mastered using acrylic on canvas.

A JOURNAL OF DREAMS AND AWAKENINGS

Heaven and Earth

Flavia and Lisa Weedn
Illustrated by Flavia Weedn

Cedco Publishing Company • San Rafael, California

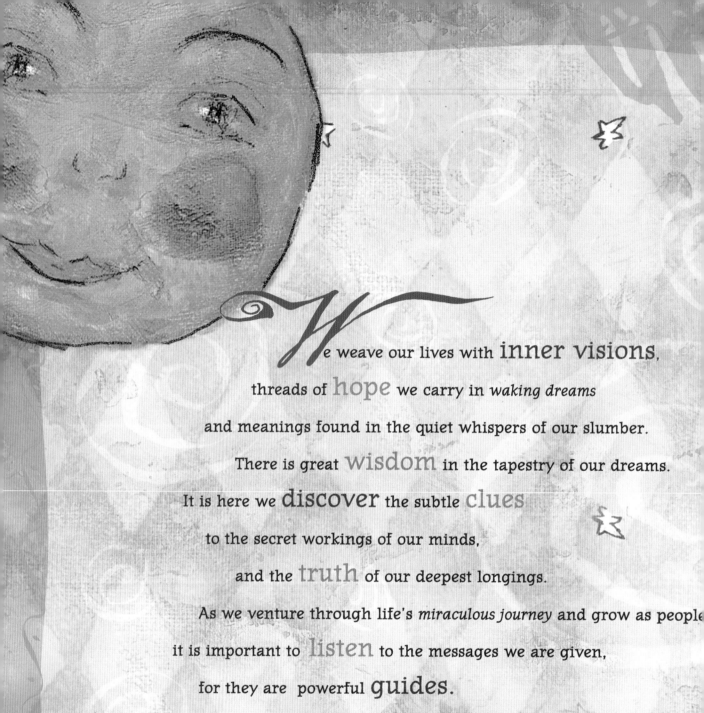

We weave our lives with inner visions,

threads of hope we carry in *waking dreams*

and meanings found in the quiet whispers of our slumber.

There is great wisdom in the tapestry of our dreams.

It is here we discover the subtle clues

to the secret workings of our minds,

and the truth of our deepest longings.

As we venture through life's *miraculous journey* and grow as people

it is important to listen to the messages we are given,

for they are powerful guides.

Every thought has its reason for surfacing;

every goal must begin with the seed of a dream.

Indeed, it is *never easy* reaching for dreams,

but those who reach surely walk in stardust.

This journal is a private place to record your inspirations,

beliefs and passions. As you climb the ladder to the stars,

it is our hope that life will reveal to you

its greatest mystery — that dreams, whether experienced

under the harvest moon or by the light of day,

are each a canvas upon which you, and you alone,

have the freedom to create your masterpiece.

May these pages become your friend, a companion along the way,

reminding you that miracles are always within your grasp

and every dream you dream can be

your reality.

Flavia

Table of Contents

From Sunrise To Starry, Starry Night

Soul Dancing
Night and Day
The Language of Dreams
Magical Metaphors
Bridges of Time
Closing the Distance
Stepping Stones
To Wisdom
Rippling Waters
Oceans of Thought
Life's Journey
Pathways and Passages

Lifeposts of Learning

New Directions
Accepting Change
Clarity of Vision
Opening My Heart
Lifting the Mask
Shedding the Armor
New Meanings
Possibilities
Being Receptive
Welcoming Knowledge
Creating the Masterpiece
The Color of Dreams

Living The Dream

Celebrating Life
Honoring the Soul
Living with Intention
Listening with Grace
Life Balance
Simplification
Prioritizing
What Really Matters
Giving Thanks
Offering Praise
Becoming More
Ladder to the Stars

When I pause to explore the

intricacies that make up the

person I am, I behold the threads of

color which create my tapestry.

The vibrant hues and dimensional texture

of my soul reveal a higher understanding.

By defining my beliefs, my passions, my view of self

and others, magic unfolds.

Here is where I find the tools to unlock my heart,

to encourage growth and healing,

and to turn the fancy of dream-thought into

vivid reality.

The Dawn of Awakenings

The Voice of My Soul

My Truths and Beliefs

Date:

Place:

Values and Ideals

Hopes and Passions

Life is a

symphony of

meaning, and

we conduct

the band.

Date:

Place:

Mind and Heart

Date: ....

Place: ....

The Looking Glass

Reflections of Self

To be

imperfectly

perfect is the

essence of

true beauty.

Date:

Place:

The Roles I Play

The Real Me

Date: _____

Place: _____

Unfinished Chapters

Places to Heal

Time is

a friend,

a healer,

a maker of

dreams.

Date:

Place:

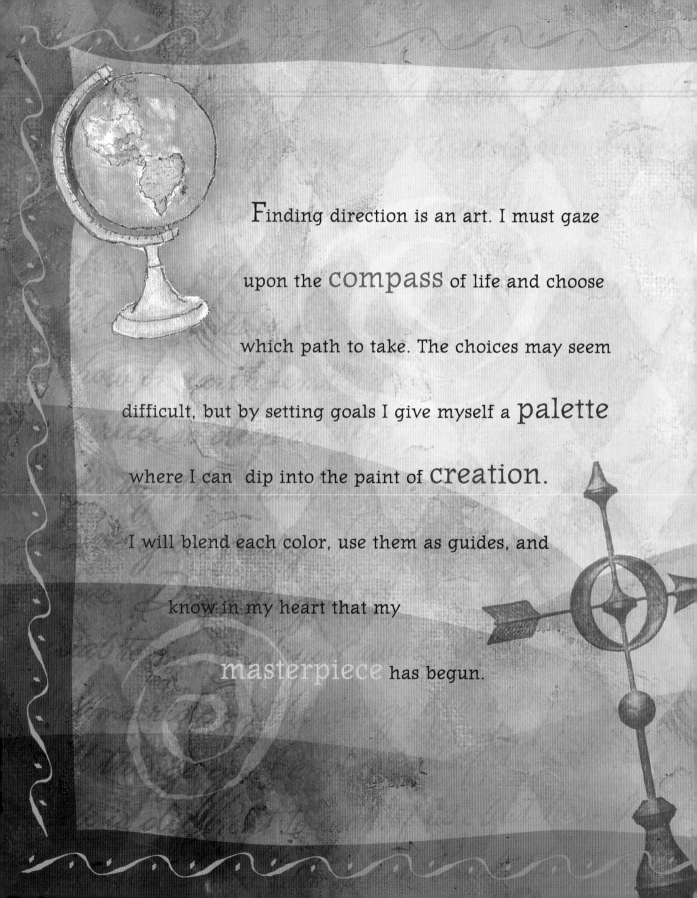

Finding direction is an art. I must gaze

upon the compass of life and choose

which path to take. The choices may seem

difficult, but by setting goals I give myself a palette

where I can dip into the paint of creation.

I will blend each color, use them as guides, and

know in my heart that my

masterpiece has begun.

Life's Compass

SKETCH

Setting Goals

Acting With Purpose

Date: .... Place: ....

Personal Relationships

Love, Friends and Family

To love and to be loved is life's greatest reward.

Date:

Place:

Touch of Faith

Prayer and Meditation

Date: ....

Place: ....

Making a Difference

Giving Back

Give all you

have to give;

even the slightest

touch may mean

more than you

dare to think.

Date:

Place:

Magic at Work

Secret Longings

Date:

Place:

Believing In Myself

Issues of Trust

When we

believe in

ourselves, we can

make anything

happen.

Date:

Place:

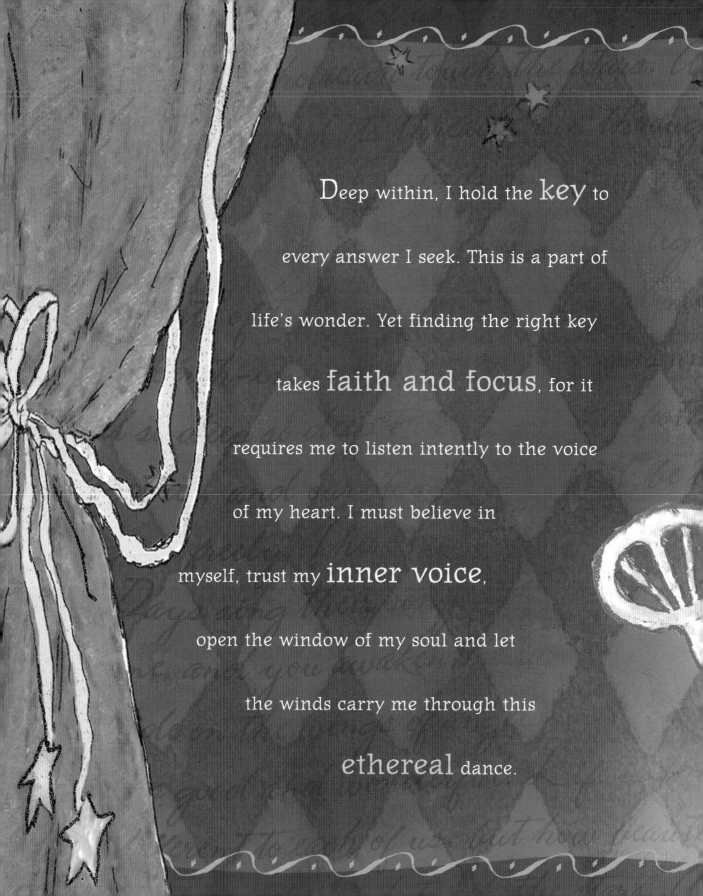

Deep within, I hold the key to

every answer I seek. This is a part of

life's wonder. Yet finding the right key

takes faith and focus, for it

requires me to listen intently to the voice

of my heart. I must believe in

myself, trust my inner voice,

open the window of my soul and let

the winds carry me through this

ethereal dance.

Unlocking
Doors,
Opening
Windows

Keys to Understanding

Listening to My Heart

Date: ....   Place: ....

Letting Go

Wings of Flight

Angels are

all around us,

and any heart

who yearns to

can reach out

and touch a

wing.

Date:

Place:

Embracing Hope

Date:

Place:

Honoring Love

Surrendering

Heaven

smiles

softly

and hears

every

wish.

Date:

Place:

Life's Timing

Destiny's Design

Date:

Place:

The Light Within

Sharing the Vision

Beautiful

people cause

beautiful

things to

happen.

Date:

Place:

The still of the night

spills stars to wish upon,

and I catch them in my dreams.

The light of day brings a beacon

of hope, and I walk the path holding

visions of what might be. In every

dream-thought my soul awakens, and I

am met with the spark of imaginings

and the promise of tomorrow.

From *Sunrise*
To *Starry,*
Starry
Night

Soul Dancing

From *Sunrise* To *Starry, Starry Night*

Soul Dancing

Night and Day

Date: ....

Place: ....

The Language of Dreams

Magical Metaphors

If we can believe in rainbows after the darkest storm, then we can believe in the reality of dreams.

Date:

Place:

Bridges of Time

Closing the Distance

Stepping Stones

Hope,

like love,

transcends all

time. It is the

song inside

your heart that

never stops

singing.

Date:

Place:

Rippling Waters

Oceans of Thought

Date: _____

Place: _____

Life's Journey

Pathways and Passages

Follow

your heart

wherever it

takes you.

Date:

Place:

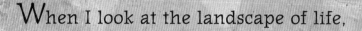

When I look at the landscape of life,

I remind myself that every day is a new beginning.

Every dawn is a chance to widen my perspective,

learn higher truths,

and take a step upward on the

ladder of my dreams.

Change is never easy, but when

I find the courage to keep

going, the gifts I am ultimately given

far outweigh the fear.

For miracles come in all shapes and sizes,

and happen to those who believe.

Lifeposts of Learning

New Directions

Accepting Change

Date: _____

Place: _____

Clarity of Vision

Opening My Heart

And

what is as

important as

knowledge?

Caring and

seeing with

the heart.

Date:

Place:

Lifting the Mask

Shedding the Armor

Date:

Place:

New Meanings

Possibilities

Nothing

is impossible

_to a_

believing

heart.

Date:

Place:

Being Receptive

Welcoming Knowledge

Date:

Place:

Creating the Masterpiece

The Color of Dreams

The

art of

creation

begins

with a

dream.

Date:

Place:

Time is a miracle woven with dreams.

Every moment matters, and it is a privilege just to

be a part of life's beauty.

Let me never forget

that I am here for a purpose,

that I have gifts to give and love

to share, and that my

contribution to the

meaning of life

is to be all I am destined to be.

Living
the Dream

Celebrating Life

Honoring the Soul

Date:

Place:

Living with Intention

Listening with Grace

The

right to

live is a

gift.

Celebrate

being

alive.

Date:

Place:

Life Balance

Date: ....

Place: ....

Prioritizing

What Really Matters

What
matters
most in life
is that we
recognize
what matters
most.

Date:

Place:

Giving Thanks

Offering Praise

Date:

Place:

Becoming More

Ladder to the Stars

If we

can love the

stars without

knowing the

vastness of the sky,

then we can

believe in the

promise of

miracles.

Date:

Place:

Flavia Weedn is one of America's leading contemporary inspirational writers and illustrators. Her work has touched the lives of millions for over three decades. Offering a kind of hope for the human spirit, Flavia portrays the basic excitement, simplicity and beauty she sees in the ordinary things of life. Lisa Weedn, Flavia's daughter and co-author, shares her mother's philosophy and passion. Their collaborative writings celebrate life and embrace meaningful core values. It is their wish to shine a beacon of hope into the lives of others by encouraging the belief that we all have a significant contribution to make in this lifetime and every dream can be realized. Their work includes numerous books, collections of fine stationery goods, giftware, and lifestyle products distributed worldwide. Flavia and Lisa live in Santa Barbara, California.